SoJaDe's
Five W's and How for Independent Authors

~

A Self-Publishing Guide for Writing with Clarity, Crafting with Purpose, and Capturing Readers

By International Best-Selling Author
Dr. Sonya Howell Barrow

SoJaDe Publishing, LLC

Cover design and graphics by:
Dr. Sonya Howell Barrow

The SoJaDe Group, LLC

Disclaimer

The content of this book is inspired by the author's methods developed and used throughout her own writing and publishing journey. This personal guidebook is provided for educational and informational purposes only. The publisher and author make no guarantees regarding results or outcomes based on the use of this material.

While the author is thrilled to share her personal experiences, insights, and lessons learned as a published author, **SoJaDe's Five W's and How for Independent Authors ~ A Self-Publishing Guide for Writing with Clarity, Crafting with Purpose, and Capturing Readers** is presented as a simple framework designed to help future independent authors gain clarity and direction in their writing process. However authors remain responsible for their own publishing decisions, the accuracy of their content, and compliance with applicable laws and guidelines.

By using this guide the reader understands and acknowledges acceptance of this disclaimer and agrees to release the publisher and author from any and all claims or causes of action, known or unknown, arising from the use of the information contained within this book.

Please enjoy.

Dedication

To my sons, Jacques and DeShon Jr., whose love, encouragement, and belief in me continues to light my path. You remind me daily of the power of perseverance and purpose.

To every independent author daring to write, determined to publish, and destined to inspire, motivate, encourage, or entertain, this guide is for you. May it serve as your blueprint, your compass, and your daily reminder that your story matters.

The world is unknowingly waiting for your words. May you write with clarity, craft with purpose, capture the hearts of readers, and let your legacy live on.

Writing with Clarity. Crafting with Purpose. Capturing Readers.

SoJaDe's
Five W's and How for Independent Authors

~

A Self-Publishing Guide for Writing with Clarity, Crafting with Purpose, and Capturing Readers

By International Best-Selling Author
Dr. Sonya Howell Barrow

SoJaDe Publishing, LLC

Every independent author carries
a blueprint within, a design for words,
a vision for stories, and a hope for
impact. Independence in writing is not
just about doing everything alone. It is
about owning your vision, embracing
your responsibility, and committing to the
process. By writing with **clarity**, crafting
with **purpose**, and capturing **readers**,
your words can live beyond you. Writing
a book is not just a dream. It is a
commitment to yourself, to your readers,
and to the lasting legacy only your
written voice can leave behind.

*~ **Dr. Sonya Howell Barrow***
SoJaDe Publishing, LLC

Table Of Contents

A Letter To My **Aspiring Author**

Dear Aspiring Author,

Writing and publishing a book is one of the most rewarding journeys you can take, but it is also one of the most demanding. Too often, aspiring authors believe the process will be quick, easy, or even free. The perception is very different and it is not the reality. Writing takes focus, editing takes skill, and publishing takes investment. All of these things require time and money.

This guide was created to help you see both the vision and the reality. You do not need to know everything at once, but you do need to commit. Your time, energy, and effort will shape the book you bring into the world.

Remember:
No one else can write your story. Others may guide you, but the responsibility and the reward will always belong to you.

With gratitude,
~ Dr. Sonya Howell Barrow
SoJaDe Publishing, LLC

Every book begins with a question, and every author begins with the courage to answer it. Write bravely, publish boldly, and leave a legacy only your voice can create.

~ *Dr. Sonya Howell Barrow*

SECTION 1:

Independent Author
and
Self-Publishing
Fundamentals

Independent "Indie" Author

An independent, or "indie," author is a writer who takes full ownership of their creative and publishing journey. Independence is not about doing everything alone. It is about making the decisions that shape your book and standing firmly behind them with confidence.

As an indie author, you choose your partners, your platforms, and your process. You hold the vision for your work and the responsibility to see it through. This independence gives you freedom, flexibility, and control. However, it also requires commitment, clarity, and direction.

Being an indie author is more than a title, it is a mindset. It means embracing the role of writer and entrepreneur/authorpreneur, understanding that your words are your product, and your voice is your brand.

Remember:
An indie author does not wait for permission. Instead they boldly create their own path and build their own legacy.

Self-Publishing

Self-publishing is the process most indie authors use to bring their books to life. Unlike traditional publishing, where the company manages every stage throughout the entire process, i.e. editing, design, printing, and distribution, self-publishing allows indie authors to directly manage/oversee these steps themselves.

Self-publishing often includes:

- Choosing your publishing platform such as Barnes & Noble Press, Amazon Kindle Direct Publishing (KDP), IngramSpark, etc.

- Establishing your own professional services that are needed for editing, cover design, and formatting.

- Setting up your distribution and determining how readers will access your book.

Self-publishing is not simple and definitely not free. It requires dedicated investment of your time, money, resources. etc. But the reward is undeniable: greater creative ideas and control, faster publishing timelines, and the ability to own your rights and royalties from the very beginning.

Remember:
Self-publishing is not just about being able to do everything alone. It is about owning the process, moving on your terms, and creating a strategy that keeps you in control.

**Being an
Independent Author
is the MINDSET.**

**Self-Publishing
is the METHOD.**

Together, they empower you
to be writing, crafting, capturing,
publishing, and sharing your
story on your own terms.

SECTION 2:

Your **Author** Journey

Welcome to Your
Author Journey

Welcome! I am excited you have chosen to take the next step in your writing journey. Writing a book is one of the most powerful and rewarding ways to share your story, your knowledge, and your vision with the world.

Writing with clarity, crafting with purpose, and capturing readers began as a framework my oldest heartbeat and I created. It helped me to gain clarity, organize my thoughts, and stay focused throughout my writing and publishing process for each of my books. I realized this particular framework could help other aspiring authors with limited experience and a tight budget.

Now I am sharing my framework to provide guidance as you embark on your own writing and publishing journey. Ultimately, you will be able to move forward with confidence and without feeling overwhelmed by costs or complicated systems.

This guide will encourage you to think deeply about your purpose, your audience, and your goals as you tell your story. Whether you are writing fiction, nonfiction, memoir, or self-help, this guide will help provide clarity and structure. Then you will confidently transform your ideas from written thoughts to a purposeful, published book.

Remember:
You do not need to have all of the answers right away. Take your time. Revisit the questions detailed within this guide as often as you need to and allow this process to refine your vision. Every author's journey is unique. This guide is here to help you make yours both intentional and achievable.

I am honored to walk alongside you on your author journey. **Let us begin!**

This Guide

Congratulations on taking the first step toward clarity, purpose, and capturing readers on your path towards publishing success. This guide is a practical framework to help you shape your ideas, clarify your message, strengthen your purpose, and define your audience.

It is intentionally formatted without lined pages so you can adapt it to your own process. Use a notebook, journal, or digital document to record answers and reflections. Keeping this guide clean and handy allows you to return to it often and apply it to future projects again and again. Whether you are writing fiction, non-fiction, self-help, memoir, or another genre, the **Five W's** and **How** can be applied consistently to guide your writing.

Remember:
Think of this guide as a flexible writing tool: it adapts to your needs while ensuring your story connects with the readers who need it most.

💡 Tip:

Create a dedicated
Author Journal to record
your answers, new ideas,
reflections, and brainstorming
notes in one place. It will
become your personal roadmap
as you move through this
guide and beyond.

Getting Started

Before we explore the **Five W's,** it is important to pause, reflect, and clarify your intentions as a published author. Writing and publishing a book is not only a commitment of time and energy, but also purpose. Therefore, the way you answer the following questions will shape how you approach this guide and your writing journey.

Now, take a moment to think about these **three thought-provoking questions:**

1. Do you want to **write** books?

2. Do you want to **sell** books?

3. Do you want to **write** and **sell** books?

Your answers may seem simple, but they carry weight. They reveal your motivation, your goals, and the direction of your publishing journey. There is no right or wrong answer. Only the answer that best reflects what you want at this stage of your author journey.

Your answers reveal the path ahead because:
- **Write:** If you want to write books that do not answer the **Five W's** and **How,** then you are probably writing books as a hobby.

  Without clarity, your words may lack focus, leaving your readers uninterested.

- **Sell:** If you want to sell books, then you need to understand the fundamentals of the **Five W's** and **How**.

  Readers buy books that feel purposeful, relevant, and focused on their needs or desires, not books that ramble without a clear message.

- **Write and Sell:** If you want to write and sell books, then you need to not only understand the **Five W's** and **How** but also understand the audience you want to sell your books to and why your message matters to them.

  - **Ask yourself:** Are your books designed to appeal to a specific race, creed, color, or origin? If not, consider using inclusive and universally appealing language and visuals for your books to prevent them from unintentionally limiting your audience.

Books that entertain, educate, and meet readers at the right time of their journey has the best chance for success.

The **Five W's** are fundamental questions, similar to those used in storytelling, journalism, and analysis. They apply across all genres: fiction, self-help, memoir, and more. But the way they are applied will differ depending on the genre.

Keep your answers to those three questions close at hand as you move into the **Five W's and How.** They will serve as your compass, keeping you aligned with your purpose while shaping the book you are called to write.

Now that you have reflected on your intentions, you are ready to explore the framework. It is your roadmap to clarity, focus, and publishing success.

Remember:
Your purpose for writing (write, sell, or both) will guide every decision you make as an author.

SECTION 3:

The
Five W's and How
Framework

The **Five W's** and **How:**
More Than Just Writing

The **Five W's** and **How** is not just a writing tool, it is the same framework used across The SoJaDe Group, LLC and SoJaDe Publishing, LLC business models, projects, and purposes.

Why? Because it forces us to answer the question every reader, client, or audience member is silently asking: **"So what?"**

- **So, what** if you want to be an author!

- **So, what** if you write a book!

- **So, what** if you publish a book!

- **So, what! So, what! So, what!**

The answer to **so what** comes from clarity.

As an author, clarity gives your writing purpose, direction, motivation, and relevance. Without it, your words become scattered and your readers lose interest. With it, your writing takes shape, transforms into a book, and connects with the audience it was meant for. Then your book, and everything you create within it will speak directly to the people it was meant for, clearly answering their unspoken **so what.**

This is why it is critical for authors to understand the relevance of the **Five W's** and **How.** These are not just questions, they are the pathway to:

- **Writing with Clarity:** This area focuses on knowing **who** your book is for and **what** your story is about.

- **Crafting with Purpose**: This area focuses on grounding your story in **when** it takes place and **where** it unfolds.

- **Capturing Readers:** This area focuses on connecting your story through your **why** and delivering your story through your **how.**

Remember:
The **Five W's** and **How** framework is at the heart of this guide. It is not just about finishing a manuscript, it is about creating your meaningful masterpiece. More than questions, the **Five W's** and **How** will form a framework that transforms ideas into a book that truly matters.

Your Roadmap to Clarity and Purpose for Publishing Success

The **Five W's** have been used in storytelling, journalism, and analysis for many years. I have expanded this framework to also include **How,** making it a complete and practical guide for new and aspiring authors.

The **Five W's** and **How** framework you are about to explore was created especially for new and aspiring authors. It will guide you in writing with **clarity,** crafting with **purpose,** and capturing **readers.**

At a glance:

- **WHO:** Identify.

- **WHAT:** Clarify.

- **WHEN:** Establish.

- **WHERE:** Ground.

- **WHY:** Uncover.

- **HOW:** Execute.

Each of these will be explored in detail in the pages that follow. Think of them not just as questions to be answered, but as a guide you can return to throughout your writing and publishing journey.

Together, these six guiding questions will help you clarify purpose, strengthen focus, and build a strong foundation for every book project.

Remember:
The way you answer these questions will shape every decision you make, starting with the very first: **W - WHO.**

WHO

Identify your characters, readers, and connections.

WHO

Clarity begins with knowing **who**
you are writing for. Until you see
your reader clearly and understand
your target audience, your words
will never land with purpose.

~ Dr. Sonya Howell Barrow

WHO

The first step in shaping your book is knowing **who** it is about and **who** it is for. Clarity here will help give your story purpose and will ensure it connects with the right audience.

Fiction:

- Who are the main characters?

- Who is your audience / reader (fantasy, sci-fi, romance, drama, horror, etc.)?

Self-Help:

- Who is your audience / reader (professionals, service members, parents, students, children, couples, specific communities, etc.)?

- Who are the knowledgeable experts or voices lending credibility to your advice or message (if applicable)?

Memoir:

- Who is the subject of the memoir (usually the author)?

- Who will connect with this personal story?

💡 **Tip:**

The clearer you are
about your **who**, the easier
it becomes to write with
clarity and market your book
effectively. Books connect
best if readers feel seen.

Author Insight:
Understanding Your
WHO in Book Design

Who you are writing for should also influence how your book should look. A book meant to guide, inspire, or serve others should feel like it was created with the reader in mind.

- **Fiction:** Your **who** shapes tone, style, and even cover design. Romance readers expect warmth and connection, thrillers lean darker and more suspenseful, fantasy demands imaginative and/or symbolic imagery. Your audience should be able to recognize your genre at a glance and without confusion.

- **Self-Help/Journal:** Avoid using your own personal photo as the main cover. Readers want space to imagine themselves within the journey. A clean, branded, or thematic design creates that invitation. Small author photos work better on the back cover, inside flaps, or in the "About the Author" page. This allows the Author's story to add credibility without unnecessarily overshadowing the reader's imagination of the story, self-help guide, or journal.

- **Memoir/Biography:** Your photo is the story. A strong, intentional author photo on the front informs the reader of authenticity and transparency. Readers of memoirs want to connect with the person behind the words.

Remember:

Knowing your **who** not only guides your writing, but also ensures it serves the right purpose and connects with the right readers. With clarity you are able to transition to your: **W - WHAT.**

WHAT

Clarify the focus, promise,
and purpose of your book.

WHAT

Every story begins with someone brave enough to tell it. Know your who, define your **what,** and your words will always find their way to the hearts they were meant for. The value of your book is not measured by how much you write, but by **what** you choose to say. Purpose is the heartbeat of every page.

~ Dr. Sonya Howell Barrow

WHAT

Once you know who your book is for, the next step is to clarify **what** your book is truly about. The **what** defines your central conflict, message, or problem being solved. It is the heart of your story.

Fiction:

- What is the central conflict or story?

- What are the motivations, behaviors and role of each character?

- What themes are explored (survival, drama, action, love, betrayal, sci-fi, survival, etc.)?

- What drives the plot?

Self-Help:

- What problem are you solving for the reader?

- What actionable steps or advice will you be able to provide?

Memoir:

- What key events or experiences define the story?

- What life lessons, truths, or messages are revealed through these experiences?

💡 **Tip:**

A strong **what** keeps
your writing purposeful.

Always ask yourself:
What thoughts do I want
readers to carry with them
after reading my book?

Author Insight: Understanding Your WHAT in Book Design

Your **what** is more than just a summary of your book, it is the promise you are making to your readers. A clear **what,** tells readers why your story matters and **what** they will gain by turning the pages.

- **Fiction:** A strong **what** creates tension and curiosity. It keeps readers invested in how the conflict unfolds.

- **Self-Help:** A clear **what** assures readers that you understand their problem and can guide them toward a solution.

- **Memoir:** A meaning and purposeful **what** invites readers to connect with your truth while seeing their own reflections in your experiences.

Remember:
When you can clearly define your **what,** you set the stage for a book that delivers on its promise and leaves readers feeling satisfied, inspired, or transformed. Now you are ready to establish your: **W - WHEN.**

WHEN

Establish timing,
pacing, and relevance.

WHEN

The heart of your book is
defined by what it is about.
But the life of your book is built
in the **when.** Books are not
written in a moment, they are
written in moments. Discipline
creates progress, and
progress creates momentum.

~ Dr. Sonya Howell Barrow

WHEN

The **when** anchors your book's context and momentum. This helps you and your readers understand the timing of events, the pacing of transformation, and why the story matters.

Fiction:

- When does the story take place (time period, era, season, etc.)?

- When do key events occur within the plot?

Self-Help:

- When are readers most likely to face this problem or challenge?

- When should readers apply your advice to see results (immediately, long-term, step-by-step, etc.)?

- When will your content be most relevant to your audience (current, long-term, etc.)?

Memoir:

- When did the events happen?

- When will your story resonate most deeply with readers?

💡 Tip:

Timing creates urgency. Whether in storytelling or problem-solving, **when** sets the rhythm that keeps readers engaged and it ensures your book feels timely and meaningful.

Author Insight: Understanding Your WHEN in Book Design

The **when** of your book influences not just the story but the way readers experience it.

- **Fiction:** Establishing a timeline grounds your plot. Whether it is a historical era, a futuristic world, or dates, timing sets the atmosphere and shapes pacing of events.

- **Self-Help:** Timing is essential and it matters during the transformations. Are you guiding readers through an immediate quick win, or a gradual change that will benefit them for a lifetime? Setting expectations builds trust.

- **Memoir:** Timing connects past to present. Readers are not just asking **when** events happened, they want to know why those moments matter to you now. Anchoring the **when** of your story in relevance will allow readers to carry your lessons forward.

Remember:
Establishing **when** ensures the story or message matters most. It helps to create momentum and relevance, ensuring your words are impactful and meet readers at the right time. Now, you must consider your: **W - WHERE.**

WHERE

Ground your book in place, setting, and context.

WHERE

Books are built in moments,
but they live in the places
they are meant to reach. Your
words don't belong everywhere,
they belong exactly **where**
they are needed most, in the
hands of the readers who
are waiting for them.

~ Dr. Sonya Howell Barrow

WHERE

The **where** provides the backdrop for your story or message to thrive. Understanding the **where** provides readers with a sense of environment, perspective, and connection. Whether it is the physical location, emotional space, or a specific transformative event/setting, the **where** helps to ground the readers and their imaginations.

Fiction:
- Where does the story take place (city, world, environment, etc.)?

- Where do key moments or turning points happen?

Self-Help:
- Where should readers apply your advice (workplace, home, school, community, etc.)?

- Where can your book or message make the greatest impact?

Memoir:

- Where did your story take place (geography, home, community, etc.)?

- Where can readers see themselves in your experiences?

💡 **Tip:**

Setting is more than
background, it brings your
story or message to life.
The stronger your **where,**
the more immersive and
relatable your book becomes.

Author Insight: Understanding Your WHERE in Book Design

The **where** shapes how readers experience your story or message.

- **Fiction:** The setting is the background of **where** the imagination takes you. Utilizing a vivid or symbolic backdrop can transform your story. Sometimes the **where** could even act as a silent character of its own.

- **Self-Help:** The environment of the self-help application matters. Sometimes advice that feels abstract falls flat. However, advice that shows readers **where** to apply it becomes actionable.

- **Memoir:** Remembering the location anchors memory. Describing **where** allows readers to imaginatively step inside your world and see your experiences through their own lens.

Remember:
The stronger your **where,** the more immersive and relatable your book becomes to readers. Now, let us explain your: **W - WHY.**

WHY

Uncover the deeper
reason behind your book.

WHY

The strength of your message
is rooted in the strength of your
why. Without it, your book is
just words on a page. Place gives
your story context, but purpose
gives it power and together,
they create the connection your
readers are searching for.

~ Dr. Sonya Howell Barrow

WHY

The **why** is the heart of your project. It reveals your motivation as an author and the purpose your book serves for readers. A clear **why** will guide your writing and give your book lasting impact.

Fiction:
- Why do your characters make their choices?

- Why will readers feel the need to care about this story (emotional connection, suspense, themes, etc.)?

Self-Help:
- Why is this an important problem that can be helped or solved by you?

- Why should readers trust your advice (your expertise, research, success, experience, etc.) now?

- Why does your book stand out from similar titles?

Memoir:

- Why are you compelled to tell your story now (inspire, heal, educate, entertain, etc.)?

- Why should readers choose to connect with your personal experience?

💡 Tip:

Your **why** is your anchor.
When writing feels challenging,
return to your **why**. It will remind
you **why** your book matters and
keep you motivated to finish.

Author Insight: Understanding Your WHY in Book Design

Your **why** is more than inspiration or motivation, it is the anchor that carries your book from idea to impact.

- **Fiction:** A compelling **why** helps to shape character decisions and it drives the story forward. It is what keeps readers invested in the outcome.

- **Self-Help:** A strong **why** demonstrates both relevance and credibility. Most readers need to know **why** this issue matters and **why** you are the right person to guide them.

- **Memoir:** A purposeful **why** shows **why** your story matters beyond your own life. Readers are drawn to memoirs when they see universal truths reflected in their own stories and personal experiences.

Remember:
Your **why** is the heartbeat that makes your words relevant and transformative. With a clear **why,** your book becomes a message, not just words on a page. You are not just writing or selling a book, you are offering a solution, a mindset, a message, or providing entertainment. All these thoughts and questions matter to readers. So, let us show them: **H - HOW.**

HOW

Execute by turning vision into action and ideas into a plan.

HOW

Your why gives your story meaning, and your **how** gives it life. Together they transform an idea into a book, and a book into a legacy. The method is not the magic, the magic is in your commitment to finish and the courage to share your voice with the world.

~ Dr. Sonya Howell Barrow

HOW

The **how** is where ideas become an actionable plan. It defines the steps, tools, and methods that will bring your book to life. Without a clearly defined **how,** your story may remain unfinished, but with it, you create a roadmap to completion.

Fiction:
- How will you structure your story (linear, flashbacks, multiple point of views)?

- How will your characters resolve conflict and reach the conclusion?

Self-Help:
- How will you deliver your advice (framework, steps, exercises, stories)?

- How will you make your content actionable and practical?

Memoir:
- How will you organize the content of your story (chronological, thematic, or blended)?

- How will you balance your truth, memory, and storytelling?

💡 **Tip:**

Your **how** bridges vision
with reality. The clearer your
plan, the easier it will be to
stay focused, consistent, and
move your book from idea
to finished manuscript.

Author Insight: Understanding Your HOW in Book Design

The **how** is not just about tools or techniques, it is about commitment.

- **Fiction:** The way you structure and resolve your story helps to determine **how** readers experience it. A clear **how** keeps the story moving and ensures a satisfying resolution.

- **Self-Help:** The **how** transforms advice into action. Frameworks, steps, and exercises give readers a simple and practical path forward, turning ideas into measurable results.

- **Memoir:** The **how** transforms memory into a narrative. Choosing **how** to organize your story and **how** much truth to reveal helps balance authenticity with readability.

Remember:
Your **how** turns vision into action. It is the bridge from clarity and purpose to capturing

readers and leaving a lasting impact. The method is never the magic. The magic is in your willingness to finish and the courage to share your voice with the world. With your **how** in place, you now hold the full framework of the **Five W's** and **How.**

THE FIVE W'S AND HOW

Know your **who**, define your **what**, honor your **when**, ground your **where**, and embrace your **why**. Then commit to your **how.** Together, these guiding questions will transform scattered ideas into focused stories, and focused stories into lasting impact. With this foundation in place, you are ready to take your next step: **Your Path Forward.**

~ *Dr. Sonya Howell Barrow*

Publishing is not the end
of writing, it is the beginning
of sharing your story with the
world. Beyond the **Five W's**
and **How** lies the practical
path that turns your vision
into a published reality.

~ Dr. Sonya Howell Barrow

SECTION 4:

Beyond the
Five W's and **How**

A Note on Publishing Options

Whenever you are ready to take your finished manuscript into the world, you will need to decide how to publish it. For most independent authors, Print on Demand (POD) is the most affordable and practical choice.

POD allows your book to be printed only when a reader places an order. This means you do not need to buy or store large quantities of book inventory, making it budget-friendly, low-risk, and accessible to new authors.

Popular POD platforms include Amazon KDP, Barnes & Noble Press, and IngramSpark. These platforms offer global distribution opportunities. While this guide has focused mainly on helping you write your book, keep PODs in mind as the natural next step when you are ready to publish.

The following pages will take you Beyond the **Five W's** and **How** with key considerations to support your publishing journey.

💡 Tip:

Do not feel pressured to
master every publishing
option at once. Begin with the
path that feels manageable,
and build from there.
The next steps will guide
you through the basics.

Basic Publishing Requirements

What You Need to Publish Professionally:
Publishing a book is not just about writing the manuscript. To bring your work from manuscript draft to shelf-ready, you will need a few key elements. These are the building blocks every independent and aspiring author should know and understand:

- **ISBN & Barcode:** These are the unique identifiers that make your book trackable and sellable in stores and online.

- **Copyright Registration:** This is optional but highly recommended for legal protection of your work.

- **Trim Size & Page Count:** This is the book size (5x8, 6x9, 8 1/2x11, etc.) and determines the physical look and cost of your book.

- **Editing:** Various types of editing such as developmental editing, proofreading, copy editing, etc. to transform your document into a polished manuscript.

- **Formatting/Layout:** The manuscript is then prepared for print (margins, fonts, spacing) and eBook (Kindle, EPUB).

- **Cover and Graphic Designs:** These are professionally designed elements that include the front, spine, and back covers, and may also include interior graphics. They are all created to attract and engage readers.

- **Distribution Setup Platforms:** Platforms such as Amazon KDP, Barnes & Noble Press, or IngramSpark for reaching readers.

Why It Matters:
Each of these elements will potentially affect your cost and credibility as an author. Cutting corners or skipping steps can make your book look unprofessional and readers will notice.

Key Takeaway:
Understand these basic publishing requirements as you begin to plan your budget. This will help you to avoid surprises and it helps to ensure your book (digital or print) is truly shelf-ready.

💡 Tip:

Professional does not have to mean expensive but it should always mean intentional. Invest where quality matters most: editing, formatting, and cover design.

Print on Demand (POD)

What It Is:

Print on Demand (POD) means your book is printed only when a reader orders it. So, this means, no warehouses, no bulk inventory, no upfront stacks of books crowding your office or home. Platforms like Amazon Kindle Direct Publishing (KDP), Barnes & Noble Press, and IngramSpark make independent printing for authors attainable and achievable.

Why It Matters:

For new and independent authors, PODs are game-changers. It lowers the financial risk of publishing, gives your book global reach, and saves you from managing the logistics of storage and shipping.

Pros:

- There are no upfront costs for bulk printing.

- There are no hidden storage or logistical fees.

- PODs usually handle fulfillment orders (printing, customer service, shipping and delivery, etc.).

- There is global distribution through Amazon, Barnes & Noble, and other online retailers.

- There is flexibility to update manuscript files (correct errors, add revisions, refresh covers, etc.).

Cons:
- There are higher cost per copy compared to bulk offset printing.

- There are limited options for paper, trim sizes, and finishes.

- Some physical bookstores prefer not to stock POD book titles unless they are ordered through distributors like IngramSpark.

Key Takeaway:
POD empowers independent authors to publish without breaking their bank accounts. Think of it as printing made simple. This option makes it ideal for new authors and their book projects. As demand grows, you can always expand into bulk printing for higher margins.

💡 **Tip:**

Start simple. Choose one
POD platform that fits
your goals and budget,
then expand as your
author brand grows.

Publishing Costs Explained

Why Pricing Varies:

One of the most common questions new and aspiring authors ask is, **"How much does it cost to publish a book?"** The truth is that this answer varies because publishing costs depend on what you choose to handle yourself versus what you choose to outsource. Knowing the areas where money is usually spent helps you plan your publishing journey realistically.

Associated Costs:

- **Editing:** This is often the largest investment. Costs vary across publishing companies and are calculated based on the word count, type of editing, editor experience, etc.

- **Graphics and Designs:** Includes both cover design and interior layout. This cost varies. However, a professional design makes your book visually appealing and easy to read.

- **ISBN & Barcode:** Free if you use certain platforms but purchasing your own gives you full ownership and flexibility.

- **Printing & Distribution:** Print on Demand (POD) has a low upfront cost but higher per-book price. Bulk printing lowers the per-book cost but requires storage space and upfront payment.

- **Marketing & Promotion:** Ads, graphics, book trailers, launch events, vendor tables, and more. Costs vary widely depending on your author brand strategy.

Why It Matters:
Without a clear breakdown, authors may feel blindsided by these unknown expenses and may become overwhelmed. Authors may be tempted to cut corners they don't understand and assume are unnecessary. But shortcuts often lead to poor quality and readers notice. A professional-looking book requires both time and investment.

Key Takeaway:
Don't just ask, "How much does publishing a book cost?" Instead, ask: "Which areas will I invest in financially for publishing my book and which areas can I manage myself during the publishing process?" This mindset shift helps authors plan strategically, budget wisely, and publish confidently.

💡 **Tip:**

Cheap can become costly.
Cutting corners on editing or
design may save money upfront,
but it risks your credibility
and credibility is priceless.

ISBN Explained:
What Every Author Needs To Know

What It Is:

International Standard Book Number (ISBN) is a unique 13-digit identifier that makes your book trackable and sellable worldwide. Think of it as your book's fingerprint. Also, no two ISBNs are the same. Therefore, each format of your book (paperback, hardcover, eBook) requires its own ISBN.

Where to Get One:

- **U.S. Authors:** Bowker (myidentifiers.com) is the official source.

- **Other Countries:** Each country has its own ISBN agency (e.g., Nielsen in the UK, Library & Archives in Canada, etc.).

- **Free ISBNs:** Platforms like Amazon KDP or B&N Press will assign an ISBN for free.

Free vs. Purchased:
- **Free ISBNs:** Platform is listed as publisher (e.g., Amazon KDP). Authors who write books as a hobby make be ok with free ISBNs.

- **Purchased ISBNs:** You list your own imprint (e.g., SoJaDe Publishing, LLC). This is the best choice for indie authors with long-term publishing plans, professional branding, and wider distribution.

Key Takeaway:
If you plan to write just one book for fun or a hobby, a free ISBN is fine. If you plan to publish multiple books, build a brand, or sell beyond Amazon, Barnes & Noble, etc., purchasing and owning your ISBN is the smarter investment.

💡 Tip:

Own your ISBNs whenever
possible. It gives you control
over your book's identity
and flexibility across platforms.
Use trusted sources only, like
Bowker, and keep your records
organized for future projects.

Key Websites & Resources for Independent Authors

Bowker: [myidentifiers.com]

This is where you purchase ISBNs (U.S. official agency). Use this site if you want to own your ISBNs and publish under your author or brand imprint.

Amazon KDP – [kdp.amazon.com]

A free publishing platform (POD) for eBooks and print-on-demand paperbacks and hard copy books. They offer global distribution through Amazon.

IngramSpark – [ingramspark.com]

A free publishing platform (POD) distribution powerhouse for most independent authors. Especially useful if you want your book in libraries and brick-and-mortar bookstores.

Barnes & Noble Press - (B&N) Press

Self-publish and distribute your books directly through Barnes & Noble. This platform is great for reaching Nook readers and for getting your books placed in B&N's online store.

Library of Congress – [loc.gov]

Apply for a PCN (Preassigned Control Number) to catalog your book if you want it in U.S. libraries.

Copyright Office – [copyright.gov]

Register your copyright in the U.S. for legal protection of your published work.

BookBaby – [bookbaby.com]

A one-stop self-publishing service that offers editing, book design, distribution, and marketing packages for authors who prefer done-for-you solutions.

Key Takeaway:

These are just a few of the important websites and a great starting point for indie authors. They will help you to publish, protect, and distribute your book confidently while avoiding scams or unnecessary third-party traps. This is not an exhaustive list. As an author/authorpreneur, you must do your own research to find the tools and platforms that best support your goals.

💡 Tip:

Use these sites as a starting
point, not the finish line. Research
each platform, compare your options,
and choose what aligns with your
goals. A true authorpreneur builds
confidence not by knowing everything
at once, but by learning and
adapting along the way.

Final Checklist
Before You Publish

Why Ask Questions First?

Publishing is exciting. However, take a moment to recap. Before you press **"publish,"** it is wise for you to pause. Knowing the answer to a few critical questions can help you to avoid costly mistakes, wasted time, and ensures your book is ready for readers.

Final Questions to Consider:

- Is my manuscript professionally edited and proofread?

- Is my cover design polished and targeted to my specific audience?

- Have I chosen the right publishing path (POD, distribution, or bulk printing)?

- Do I understand the costs involved and where I have chosen to invest versus do-it-yourself (DIY)?

- Do I have a basic marketing or launch plan?

- Am I ready to commit the time, energy, and resources needed to support my book after it is published?

Why It Matters:
Books that are rushed to market often fall flat, not because the story is not good, but because the author skipped the preparation. Readers notice quality, and quality builds trust.

Key Takeaway:
Publishing is more than hitting a button. When you take time to answer all of these questions honestly, you position your book and yourself as an author destined for success.

💡 **Tip:**

Pausing before you publish
is not a delay, it is preparation.
A thoughtful launch always
outperforms a rushed release.

Clarity gives you direction, but
action brings your book to life.
Beyond the **Five W's** and **How**,
your publishing journey is waiting.
Every step you take carries your
words closer to the eyes, ears, and
hearts of readers who need them most.

*~ **Dr. Sonya Howell Barrow***

SECTION 5:

Your **Path** Forward

Five W's and How Across Genres

While the **Five W's** and **How** framework remain constant, the way you apply them will shift depending on your genre.

- **Fiction:** This framework will help guide you in building immersive worlds while crafting vivid, entertaining, character-driven stories that hold the reader's attention.

- **Self-help:** This framework will help you to focus on solving real problems and delivering clear, actionable steps that readers can apply to their lives.

- **Memoirs:** This framework focuses on the authenticity, relatability, and resonance with readers. This allows your story to connect on a deeply personal level.

No matter the genre, this framework will help you to create books that are designed to inspire, motivate, encourage, and entertain readers who need your words most.

💡 Final Tip
Your Author's Compass:

Always return to the three thought-provoking questions and the **Five W's** and **How** whenever you are creating your next masterpiece. They are your compass, keeping your vision clear and your storytelling intentional.

A Closing Letter To
My Aspiring Author

Dear Aspiring Author,

Time is precious, and publishing a book requires both **time and money**. Writing demands focus, editing requires skill, formatting, and design call for expertise. None of this happens freely or without commitment.

If you want your book to be more than just an idea, you must move forward with purpose and determination. No one can hand you a ready-made blueprint and then do the work for you. This framework has given you the tools. However, it will be your investment of time, money, and effort that brings your story to life and allows you to share it with the world.

As you embark on your journey as an author, remember my four author pillars: **FIRE. GLE. Soldier Girl. TEA.**

- **FIRE:** Be **fearless** in writing with passion, **inspired** to imagine new possibilities,

resilient when challenges arise, and **empowered** to let your words ignite change.

- **GLE:** Embrace **growth** as you sharpen your craft, live with **leadership** as you share your written voice, and then pursue **elevation** as you rise boldly in building your author brand.

- **Soldier Girl:** Stand with **strength** in your voice, **service** in your purpose, and **survival** in your discipline. Writing is a battle of focus and endurance, but victory belongs to those who persist.

- **TEA:** Let your words be **tantalizing** enough to capture attention, **enchanting** enough to hold your reader, and **ascending** enough to lift hearts and minds. Whether you write to inspire, motivate, encourage, or entertain, your story deserves to be savored one page at a time.

Your words are powerful but only if you are willing to invest in them. Respect the process, honor your time, your resources, and your vision. That is the true path of the independent author.

With gratitude,
~ Dr. Sonya Howell Barrow
SoJaDe Publishing, LLC

Remember:

You hold the pen in
your hand to write and tell
your story the way
you want it to be told!

~ Dr. Sonya Howell Barrow

SoJaDe's
Five W's and How for Independent Authors
~
A Self-Publishing Guide for Writing with Clarity, Crafting with Purpose, and Capturing Readers

By International Best-Selling Author
Dr. Sonya Howell Barrow

SoJaDe Publishing, LLC

Closing

Acknowledgments

No book is ever created alone. I give all thanks to God for the gift of words, the strength to persevere, and the opportunity to use my voice for encouragement.

While writing may be a solitary act, publishing is always an empowering journey made possible by the encouragement, wisdom, and support of others.

To my family, especially my children, my two heartbeats, Jacques and DeShon Jr., thank you for your love, patience, and belief in me. You gave me the space to create and the courage to keep going.

To my mentors, colleagues, and fellow authors, your insights and shared experiences have inspired me to refine my process and create a guide that I hope will light the path for others.

To the aspiring authors who will read this book, you are the reason it was written. Every question you asked, every doubt you voiced, and every dream you shared helped shape this framework. My hope is that these pages give you clarity, courage, and confidence as you step into your own independent author journey.

A Special thanks to Authorpreneur Sonya...the Soldier Girl, the dreamer, the doer, and the fighter within me who will never quit.
Once A Dream, Now The Reality!
The SoJaDe Group, LLC

With deep gratitude,
~ Dr. Sonya Howell Barrow
SoJaDe Publishing, LLC

About The Author

Dr. Sonya Howell Barrow

Dr. Sonya Howell Barrow is a retired U.S. Army Combat Veteran who served honorably and distinctively for over 26+ years in various organizations and deployments before retiring as a Chief Warrant Officer Five (CW5) in November 2018. She was born at Fort Gordon (previously known as Camp Gordon, now known as Fort Eisenhower), Georgia and raised between Augusta and Warrenton, Georgia. She is a mother of two adult sons, Jacques and DeShon Jr.

Dr. Sonya received her Doctor of Humane Letters from Mainseed Christian University (MCU) and achieved the credentials of Global Fellowship in Leadership Principles. As an Information Technology and Cyber Security professional, she earned her Master's Degree in Cyber Security from the University of Maryland, University College (now known as University of Maryland Global Campus). Since her retirement from the U.S. Army, Dr. Sonya has pursued her dream as a published author. She is an Amazon International Bestselling Author, Certified Life

Coach, Founder of Authorpreneur Sonya, CEO and Owner of The SoJaDe Group, LLC and SoJaDe Publishing, LLC.

If Dr. Sonya isn't reading, traveling, and spending time with family and friends, she is writing and motivating others by letting them know that the "glass is always half full, never half empty." With her faith, strong will, and determination, she chooses to be a beacon of hope and strives to encourage others to live their best lives that are filled with confidence, self-awareness, and personal growth. Dr. Sonya provides a creative artistic space via her social media platforms and websites to showcase her non-fiction and fiction published works spanning across four distinct pillars:

1-Inspire and Motivate: **Fearless. Inspired. Resilient. Empowered.** 🔥 **FIRE.**

2-Self-Help: **Growth. Leadership. Elevation.** ⤴ **GLE.**

3-Soldier Girl: **Military Life.** 🥾

4-Entertainment: **Tantalizing. Enchanting. Ascending.** 🍵 **TEA.**

With a diverse collection spanning across four genres, Dr. Sonya invite readers into a world of inspiration and adventure. Each published work is a testament to her passion for storytelling, delivered thoughtfully and authentically.

Igniting Your  **FIRE.**
Encouraging Your **GLE.**
Military Life **SOLDIER GIRL.**
Savoring My **TEA.**

"Inspiring, motivating, encouraging, and entertaining readers through captivating storytelling by telling one story at a time."

~ Dr. Sonya Howell Barrow

Contact Information

Contact Information

Email:
hello@sonyahowellbarrow.com

Website:
http://www.sonyahowellbarrow.com

Linktr.ee:
https://linktr.ee/sonyahowellbarrow

Facebook:
https://www.facebook.com/authorpreneursonya

Instagram:
https://www.instagram.com/authorpreneursonya

LinkedIn:
https://www.linkedin.com/in/sonyahowellbarrow/

TikTok
https://www.tiktok.com/@authorpreneursonya

Amazon Author Central:
https://www.amazon.com/stores/Sonya-Howell-Barrow/author/B0C5425D8W?

Dr. Sonya Howell Barrow

Thank You

Thank you for allowing me to be part of your author journey. Writing a book is no small task. It takes vision, courage, and persistence. By working through the **Five W's** and **How,** you have taken meaningful steps toward shaping your story and preparing your book to share with the world.

Your voice matters. Your story matters. And the world needs what only you can create.

I am honored that you chose to spend this time with my book, **SoJaDe's Five W's and How for Independent Authors ~ A Self-Publishing Guide for Writing with Clarity Crafting with Purpose, and Capturing Readers.** May this book serve as a guide, a companion, a source of encouragement, or a blueprint whenever you need to return to its pages.

Write bravely. Publish boldly. Leave your legacy.

With gratitude,
~ Dr. Sonya Howell Barrow
SoJaDe Publishing, LLC